A person's wealth was reflected in what they ate. It seems that the ancient Egyptians were better nourished than many contemporary civilizations. Egypt's strength as a culture has been in part attributed to a well nourished population. The great river Nile flooded every year in the summer and left behind a rich soil to take the seeds in November and yield a harvest in April, often giving two crops a year.

While bread and beer were the staples, most people it seems enjoyed quite a healthy diet of fish, rabbit, fowl - such as goose, duck, quail and pigeon. In addition they had eggs, dairy products, a great variety of pulses including chick peas, lentils and broad (fava) beans, vegetables, fruit, bread and beer, sweetening their food with dates and fruit juice. The better off would have also enjoyed pig, sheep and goat, using honey as a sweetener. The elite also ate wild game such as ibex, antelope and deer and drank wine made from grapes, pomegranates or plums. The most prestigious of all meat was wild cattle and beef.

The ancient Egyptians could boil, fry and roast, salt dry and probably smoke their food. Due to the climate, preserving most food would have been a high priority. Women cooked in domestic kitchens with wooden utensils, clay pots and jars, pestles and mortars and sieves, but professional cooks were men. The Egyptians had at least twenty names for oil, from sesame and safflower to flax and horseradish, as well as clarified butter and animal fats. However it seems the ancient Egyptians ate healthily and were not overweight, with only the elite wishing to be portrayed with "prosperous" rolls of fat.

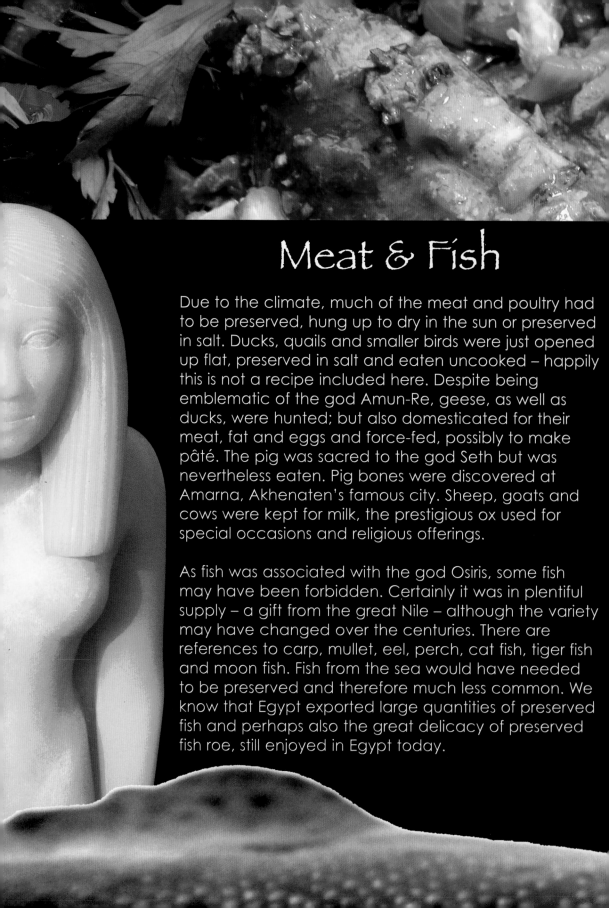

Meat & Fish

Due to the climate, much of the meat and poultry had to be preserved, hung up to dry in the sun or preserved in salt. Ducks, quails and smaller birds were just opened up flat, preserved in salt and eaten uncooked – happily this is not a recipe included here. Despite being emblematic of the god Amun-Re, geese, as well as ducks, were hunted; but also domesticated for their meat, fat and eggs and force-fed, possibly to make pâté. The pig was sacred to the god Seth but was nevertheless eaten. Pig bones were discovered at Amarna, Akhenaten's famous city. Sheep, goats and cows were kept for milk, the prestigious ox used for special occasions and religious offerings.

As fish was associated with the god Osiris, some fish may have been forbidden. Certainly it was in plentiful supply – a gift from the great Nile – although the variety may have changed over the centuries. There are references to carp, mullet, eel, perch, cat fish, tiger fish and moon fish. Fish from the sea would have needed to be preserved and therefore much less common. We know that Egypt exported large quantities of preserved fish and perhaps also the great delicacy of preserved fish roe, still enjoyed in Egypt today.

Beer & Wine

Throughout the centuries not only did the ancient Egyptians love to eat, drink and feast, but they loved to get drunk. Beer was the staple drink and probably varied from the very weak to the very potent.

Fermented from bread, wheat or barley and perhaps flavoured with malted grain it was the drink of the general population and would be the perfect accompaniment for the recipes in this book.

In ancient Egypt only the privileged would drink wine made from grapes, pomegranates or plums, so if you are feeling privileged like a pharaoh, drink wine with these recipes.

A useful tip from ancient Egypt. If you eat a lot of cabbage before you drink it will stop you being drunk! Mind you it probably only applies to ancient Egyptians.

A SELECTION OF
MEAT AND FISH
AVAILABLE IN
ANCIENT EGYPT

BEEF
CARP
DUCK
EEL
GOAT
GOOSE
HARE
LAMB
MULLET
MOON FISH
PERCH
QUAIL
PIGEON
PORK
RABBIT
TIGER FISH

Vegetables

The ancient Egyptian diet relied heavily on vegetables, with the strong tastes predominating. The ancient Egyptians loved onions and garlic and highly valued them, used them for medical purposes and believed them to be good for the health. Peas, beans, pulses, leeks, various kinds of lettuce, including endive (chicory), gourds, radishes and cucumbers were enjoyed, often with an oil and vinegar dressing. As it is today, molokhia was probably a staple vegetable. Belonging to the hemp family, the dark nourishing green, slightly bitter leaves were used very much like spinach, eaten as a vegetable or salad or used in a soup.

A SELECTION OF FRUIT & VEGETABLES AVAILABLE IN ANCIENT EGYPT

BROAD BEANS (FAVA) - VARIOUS
COURGETTES (ZUCCHINI)
CUCUMBER
DATES – FRESH OR DRIED
ENDIVE (CHICORY)
FENUGREEK
FIGS
GOURDS
GRAPES – RED & WHITE

Fruit

The climate in ancient Egypt dictated the types of fruit that could be grown and made preservation vital. Fruit varied from the range available in the early periods to a wider selection introduced during Ptolemaic and Roman times. Dates, sycamore figs, pomegranates, persea, melons and grapes have all been known since earliest times. Mulberries were also known although pears, cherries and peaches were not introduced until the Roman period. Red grapes were preferred for eating, fresh or dried as raisins, and also for red wine, whilst the white variety seems to have been mostly used for wine. Citrus fruits, in particular lemons, were not known in pharaonic times, so the earlier cooks had to make do with sour wine or vinegar to add acidity.

Generally it seems, the ancient Egyptians enjoyed a healthy variety of fruit and vegetables as the archaeological evidence suggests.

A SELECTION OF
FRUIT &
VEGETABLES
AVAILABLE IN
ANCIENT EGYPT

LEEKS
MARROW
(LIKE ZUCCHINI)
MELONS
MOLOKHIA
MULBERRIES
NEBES BERRIES
ONIONS
PAPYRUS
PERSEA
PLUMS
(DAMASCUS)
POMEGRANATES
RADISH
WATER MELON

Condiments

Condiments were always valued in ancient times to enhance the flavour of what were, to our modern palate, basic and rather uninteresting staple ingredients. The ancient Egyptians were no exception, but fascinatingly many of the flavours that they enjoyed are used today in modern Egyptian cuisine. Cinnamon, cumin, coriander (cilantro), mint, sesame and garlic are still very popular today.

Apart from the herbs and spices available, it is highly probable that fragrances obtained from flowers were used as flavourings, as is found in some Middle Eastern cooking today. Roses are known to have been grown in ancient Egypt and the ancient Egyptians were experts in creating unguents, so it is reasonable to assume that rose essence was used in cooking adding an exotic flavour. If used, it was probably restricted to the tables of the elite.

Certain foods however, appear to have been luxury items. Nuts such as almonds and walnuts were imported items and mostly enjoyed by the privileged.

Bread

There are references to 'grain' from the very earliest times. Whether the ancient 'emmer' wheat or barley, grain was the food of everyday life. Not only was it a staple food but a currency for wages and trade, as well as essential for religious offerings in temples and tombs.

Bread appears in all shapes and sizes, formed by hand or moulded in pottery moulds, leavened or unleavened. It was baked in ovens, on hot stones or open fires or steamed.

The simplest form, eaten by the average person, was a kind of pitta bread, unleavened and made with barley flour. The richer and more sophisticated would be able to choose loaves in a wide variety of shapes and sizes, probably made from 'emmer' wheat and flavoured with nuts, fruits such as dates and spices such as cumin. Only the finest breads were used as offerings and piled high in tombs to be enjoyed in the afterlife.

However, for some purposes the dried tuber of the prolific papyrus, a member of the sedge family, known today as 'tiger nuts' or chufa would have been ground and used as a flour, for cakes as pastries.

Bread is the perfect accompaniment for the meat, fish and vegetable dishes in this book. There are no bread recipes here as breads, easily purchased today, are, if carefully selected, perfectly acceptable for an ancient Egyptian meal. The flour used in these recipes is either barley flour for its flavour or grain flour from chick peas, for its texture.

THE RECIPES

No "recipes" as such have survived from ancient Egypt. The recipes in this book are based on archaeological and historical evidence. They have been created using ingredients known to have been available in ancient Egypt and influenced by dishes from historical times. They are as far as possible what one might expect to have been placed on the table of a pharaoh such as Tutankhamun.

SETI'S VEGETABLE BAKES

Makes approx 12

INGREDIENTS

150 g / 6 oz fresh or frozen broad (fava) beans - cooked.
100 g / 4 oz feta cheese.
1 egg – beaten.
75 g / 3 oz sesame seeds.
25 g / 1 oz fine breadcrumbs.
1 aubergine (egg plant).
1 onion – finely chopped.
1 leek – washed and finely chopped.
1 clove garlic – finely chopped.
1 heaped teaspoon dill seeds.
1 – 2 tablespoons olive oil.
2¼ teaspoons salt.

METHOD

- Heat oven to 200°C / fan 180°C gas mark 6.
- Slice aubergine thickly, sprinkle with 2 teaspoons salt, stand for 15 minutes, rinse and dry, then fry gently in 1 tablespoon oil until browned on both sides. Set aside.
- In same pan add ½ tablespoon oil and gently fry dill, onion, leek and garlic until soft.
- In a processor combine beans and onion mixture until blended but still coarse.
- Coarsely chop aubergines and add with ¼ teaspoon salt and egg. Add breadcrumbs if too moist.
- Cut feta into centimetre / ½ inch cubes and cover with mixture to form a ball.
- Coat in sesame seeds and place on a non - stick sheet.
- Bake until golden brown - approx 20 - 30 mins.

Delicious warm or cold served with salad for a light meal or starter.

KARNAK BEAN SALAD

serves approx 4

INGREDIENTS

200 g / 8 oz dried broad (fava) beans.
2 sticks lemon grass.
1 tablespoon olive oil.
1 teaspoon cumin seeds.
Bunch of spring onions (scallions) - chopped.
Salt to taste.
Vegetable stock or water.
Quail eggs – hard boiled.
Salad leaves.

METHOD

• Soak beans overnight, drain, rinse then cover with stock, add lemon grass and cumin. Simmer until beans are soft, approximately 1 hour. Drain.
• Remove lemon grass and mix with oil, salt and spring onions.
• Serve with salad leaves and hard boiled quail eggs.

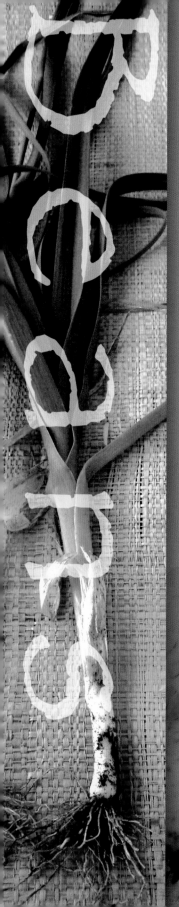

is dish has been known in
ypt since ancient times
d is still popular
day. If you want
cheat use fresh
frozen broad
va) beans
d the juice
a lemon.

LEAVES OF MEMPHIS
Warm Courgette Salad

INGREDIENTS

Courgettes (zucchini) for four people.
1 tablespoon date syrup.
1 tablespoon vinegar.
2 tablespoons olive oil.
Butter for frying.
1 tablespoon red wine.
1 tablespoon Thai fish sauce.
1 teaspoon ground cumin.
½ teaspoon ground
coriander (cilantro).
1 bunch mint – finely chop
Salt to taste.

METHOD

• Put all the ingredients
except the courgettes in a
sealed container. Shake we
• Slice the courgettes and fry
in butter until cooked to taste
• Drizzle with dressing and serve

Vegetables in the gourd family, including marrows and courgettes have been eaten in Egypt since antiquity.

Stuffed Cabbage Leaves

makes approx 8

INGREDIENTS

1 Savoy or similar cabbage.
125 g / 5 oz spinach.
40 g / 1½ oz raisins.
1 tablespoon sesame oil.
1 clove garlic - crushed.
1 small onion - finely chopped.
½ teaspoon celery seeds.
280 ml / ½ pt stock.
cocktail sticks.

METHOD

• Remove tough outer leaves. Select approximately 10 leaves and blanch quickly in boiling water. Drain and refresh in cold water.
• Fry garlic, onion, celery seeds and raisins gently in oil to soften. Add spinach and mix. Cool slightly, divide into 8 portions.
• Cut hardest stalk from cabbage leaves and place portion of filling on each leaf. Fold in side edges and roll, securing with cocktail stick.
• Return rolls to pan, add stock and simmer uncovered for a few minutes until cooked to taste.
• Remove from stock, take out cocktail sticks.
• Serve warm.

These stuffed leaves are delicious served with meat dishes or even fish. Cabbage like Savoy is ideal as the leaves roll easily and the pale colour contrasts wonderfully with the darkness of the stuffing.

AMARNA PORK

serves approx 4

INGREDIENTS

Cut of pork of your choice.
3 tablespoons honey.
1 tablespoon yogurt.
1 tablespoon sesame oil.
½ teaspoon vinegar.
1 clove garlic - crushed.
½ teaspoon black onion seeds.
1 teaspoon ground cinnamon.
¼ teaspoon salt.

METHOD

• Mix all ingredients together to make a marinade.
• Pierce pork and cover in marinade, refrigerate for several hours or overnight.
• Cook pork slowly, checking to avoid burning and add surplus marinade throughout cooking.

Pork bones were found in abundance at Amarna, the site of Akhenaten's famous city. This marinade is perfect for any cut of pork, preferably cooked slowly.

pork

NILE FOWL WITH POMEGRANATE

Serves 4

This recipe uses the brown, syrupy pomegranate "molasses" that can be found in Middle Eastern stores or some supermarkets and is well worth discovering. It is delicious made with any fowl cut into portions, although it is easier to eat if these are boneless.

INGREDIENTS

8 pieces duck, pheasant or other fowl.
200 g / 8 oz walnuts – finely chopped.
1 onion – finely chopped.
1 clove garlic – finely chopped.
1 large cinnamon stick.
1 tablespoon olive oil.
1 teaspoon ground coriander.
420 ml / ¾ pt stock or water.
3 tablespoons pomegranate molasses.
Salt to taste.
1 pomegranate to garnish (optional).
Fresh coriander to garnish (optional).

METHOD

- Brown fowl pieces in oil, remove and set aside.
- Add onion and gently brown.
- Add cinnamon, garlic, coriander and walnuts and cook gently for a few minutes.
- Add pomegranate molasses and stock and bring slowly to the boil.
- Return fowl, cover and simmer for about 30 minutes, then uncover and continue cooking until the meat is thoroughly cooked and the sauce is thick and glossy – between 10 and 20 minutes.
- Add salt to taste.
- Cut pomegranate in two horizontally (if using), remove fleshy seeds and use to garnish with fresh coriander.
- Serve immediately with nan or pitta bread.

Pomegrane

LAMB OF HORUS

serves 4

INGREDIENTS

750 g / 1¾ lbs lean diced lamb.
1 onion - sliced.
2 cloves garlic - crushed.
250 ml / ½ pt pomegranate juice.
12 soft, stoned prunes plus a few to finish.
2 teaspoons rosemary.
1 teaspoon ground coriander (cilantro).
1 tablespoon olive oil.
250 ml / ½ pt stock.
Yogurt to finish.
Fresh coriander (cilantro) to garnish.

METHOD

• Fry onion, garlic and coriander in oil.
• Add the lamb in small batches to enable it to brown.
• Add pomegranate juice, stock, rosemary and prunes, bring to a simmer.
• Cover and simmer gently until the meat is cooked (at least 1 hr) and the sauce is thickened to your taste.
• Serve accompanied by nan or pitta bread, garnished with extra prunes and coriander and drizzled with yogurt.

FOWL OF ATUM

serves 4

THE BIRD.

Remove the giblets, wash cavity well and sprinkle with salt. Stuff with mixture. Roast according to weight but allow extra time as the bird is stuffed. Make sure that the stuffing, that contains raw pork, is thoroughly cooked.

For a simpler version use the stuffing with boneless breasts. Slit, stuff and reseal. Place on greased aluminium foil and bake. The stuffing also makes an excellent starter in the form of 'Tut' burgers baked or fried. Serve these with salad leaves topped with a fried quail egg.

THE STUFFING.

100 g /4 oz ground pork.
1 onion - finely chopped.
1 leek - washed and finely chopped.
100 g /4 oz raisins.
25 g / 1 oz sesame seeds dry fried.
25 g / 1 oz breadcrumbs.
2 dessertspoons sesame oil.
1 tablespoon honey.
2 cloves of garlic - crushed.
¼ teaspoon salt.
2 teaspoons ground fennel.
1 teaspoon rose essence for the exotic version.

• Fry onion, leek, garlic and fennel in sesame oil until soft.
• Cool slightly, then add other ingredients and mix well.
• Use immediately.

The Egyptians were very fond of fowl. This recipe works well with most kinds of poultry and game birds. The fennel stuffing is excellent but for a more exotic taste, add a little rose essence

MENNA'S FISH

Fish are frequently depicted on tomb paintings. Fresh fish would have had to be processed quickly; so dried, pickled or salted fish would have been far more practical in the hot climate.

For this recipe use a fresh fish such as mullet, however almost any fish can be used. Thai fish sauce is the nearest modern equivalent to the "garum" of antiquity, which was probably a pungent fermented fish stock. To best compliment the fish, choose from the three classic sauces below, believed in Roman times to be ancient Egyptian.

Sauce One

The darkest and thickest of the sauces, it is also very good with poultry or game birds.

6 soft stoned prunes.
1 teaspoon dried onion.
1 teaspoon dried oregano.
1 teaspoon celery seeds.
1 teaspoon Thai fish sauce.
1 dessertspoon olive oil.
1 dessertspoon red wine.
9 fluid oz vegetable stock or water.

• Mix all the ingredients in a blender. Simmer for a few minutes, serve hot with the fish.

Sauce Two

2 soft stoned prunes.
6 stalks fresh coriander (cilantro) – chopped.
1 teaspoon dried onion.
1 teaspoonful celery seeds.
1 teaspoon Thai fish sauce.
1 dessertspoon red wine.
1 dessertspoon olive oil.
4 fluid oz vegetable stock or water.

• Mix all the ingredients in a blender. Simmer for a few minutes, serve hot with the fish.

Sauce Three

This sauce is the palest, lightest and most delicate of the sauces.

100 g / 4 oz white seedless grapes
6 stalks fresh coriander (cilantro) – chopped.
½ teaspoon celery seeds.
1 teaspoon Thai fish sauce.
1 dessertspoon olive oil.
4 fluid oz water or white wine.

• Mix all the ingredients in a blender. Simmer for a few minutes, serve hot with the fish.

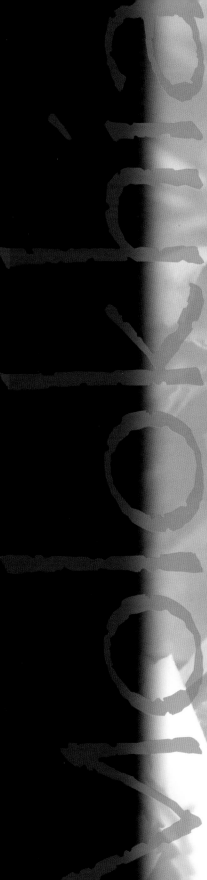

MOLOKHIA OMELETTE

Makes 4 omelettes

Unlike conventional omelettes this recipe relies on the eggs not being beaten to make rolling successful.

INGREDIENTS

8 eggs.
6 g / ¼ oz dried molokhia leaves or good handful fresh spinach thoroughly washed and coarsely chopped.
1 tablespoon coarsely ground coriander (cilantro).
50 g / 2 oz raisins.
50 g / 2 oz pine nuts.
1 leek - washed and chopped.
2 tablespoons olive oil.
Bunch mint - chopped (leave some for garnish).
Yogurt and salad for accompaniment.

METHOD

• If using dried molokhia leaves simmer gently in a little stock for 10 minutes to rehydrate. Drain.
• Put 1 tablespoon oil in pan, add coriander and pine nuts and fry gently for 1 minute. Add leek and fry gently until just soft.
• Cool, then add molokhia or spinach and mint. Mix. Divide into 4 portions.
• Lightly mix 2 eggs with a fork and in a hot pan put a little oil and add eggs, tilting pan to cover base.
• Quickly sprinkle 1 portion of vegetable mix evenly over eggs, reduce heat and roll omelette.
• Repeat until mixture is used up, keeping made omelettes warm.
• Serve immediately with yogurt and salad.

PHARAOH'S FIGS

serves 4

This dish is best served warm but also good cold with natural yogurt. It can be made beforehand and keeps well in the fridge.

INGREDIENTS

14 soft dried figs.
4 dessertspoons acacia honey.
16 dessertspoons red wine.
2 cinnamon sticks.
1 teaspoon ground caraway seeds.

METHOD

• Prick each fig with a fork.
• Place in pan large enough to keep the figs intact, add cinnamon and just enough water to cover.
• Gently simmer uncovered for 30 minutes. The figs should be swollen, soft and whole.
• Remove from liquid, discard cinnamon sticks, reserve liquid.
• In same pan add remaining ingredients and pulpy seeds from 2 of the figs and 8 dessertspoons of the reserved liquid. Mix well.
• Return figs to pan and simmer gently for 8-12 minutes or until syrup has reduced and thickened.

Inspired by the perfume of a pharaoh's garden, these delightful little cookies are quick and easy to make and are delicious on their own or with fruit compote and / or ice cream, which Tutankhamun would have loved!

BELOVED OF SELKIT

Makes approx 21

INGREDIENTS

50 g / 2 oz barley flour.
50 g / 2 oz unsalted butter.
100 g / 4 oz ground almonds.
25 g / 1 oz honey.
1 egg.
2 teaspoons rose essence*.
2 teaspoons almond oil*.
24 unskinned almonds for decoration.

METHOD

• Heat oven to 180°C / 160°C fan / gas mark 4.
• Sieve flour, add the almonds and mix.
• Melt butter, cool slightly, then add honey and egg and beat with a fork.
• Make a well in the flour and add the honey mixture.
• Mix well.
• Add rose essence and almond oil. Mix well.
• Roll one teaspoon of mixture into a ball, place on a non - stick or baking parchment lined tray.
• Push an unskinned almond firmly on top of each ball.
• Bake for 20 minutes or until golden brown.

* The rose essence used here can be found in small bottles in good supermarkets. Not to be confused with rose water which is much less concentrated and not suitable here.
*Almond oil is available in good supermarkets. Ordinary almond essence could be used but the result is not as good.

Rose and almond

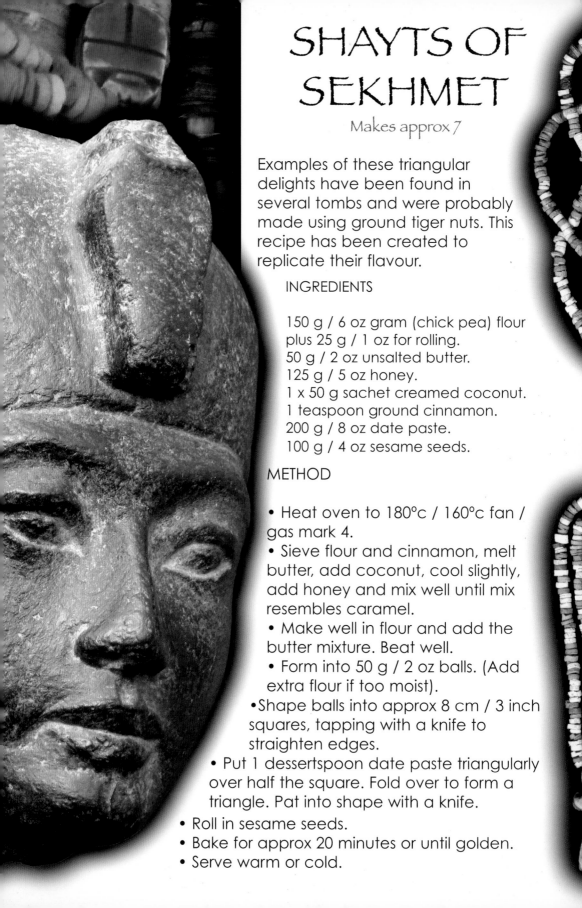

SHAYTS OF SEKHMET

Makes approx 7

Examples of these triangular delights have been found in several tombs and were probably made using ground tiger nuts. This recipe has been created to replicate their flavour.

INGREDIENTS

150 g / 6 oz gram (chick pea) flour plus 25 g / 1 oz for rolling.
50 g / 2 oz unsalted butter.
125 g / 5 oz honey.
1 x 50 g sachet creamed coconut.
1 teaspoon ground cinnamon.
200 g / 8 oz date paste.
100 g / 4 oz sesame seeds.

METHOD

• Heat oven to 180°c / 160°c fan / gas mark 4.
• Sieve flour and cinnamon, melt butter, add coconut, cool slightly, add honey and mix well until mix resembles caramel.
• Make well in flour and add the butter mixture. Beat well.
• Form into 50 g / 2 oz balls. (Add extra flour if too moist).
• Shape balls into approx 8 cm / 3 inch squares, tapping with a knife to straighten edges.
• Put 1 dessertspoon date paste triangularly over half the square. Fold over to form a triangle. Pat into shape with a knife.
• Roll in sesame seeds.
• Bake for approx 20 minutes or until golden.
• Serve warm or cold.

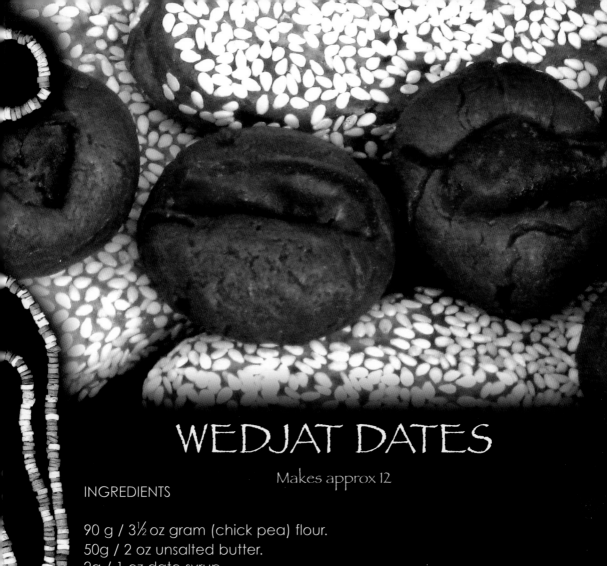

WEDJAT DATES

Makes approx 12

INGREDIENTS

90 g / 3½ oz gram (chick pea) flour.
50g / 2 oz unsalted butter.
2g / 1 oz date syrup.
¼ teaspoon ground cumin.
½ teaspoon ground cinnamon.
75 g / 3 oz date paste.
6 dates.

METHOD

- Heat oven to 180°c / 160°c fan / gas mark 4.
- Sieve flour, cinnamon and cumin.
- Melt butter then add date paste and date syrup, mix well.
- Make a well in the middle of flour and add butter mixture.
- Mix into a marzipan - like paste and roll into walnut sized balls.
- Place on non - stick tray.
- Cut dates in half length ways and press into each ball.
- Bake for approximately 25 minutes.

Cinnamon